DEMOCRACY –
A WORK IN PROGRESS

AN IRREVERENT EXERCISE
IN POLITICAL THOUGHT

Ernest Lamers

SOCIETAS
essays in political
& cultural criticism

imprint-academic.com

Published in the UK by
Imprint Academic Ltd., PO Box 200, Exeter EX5 5YX, UK

Distributed in the USA by
Ingram Book Company,
One Ingram Blvd., La Vergne, TN 37086, USA

ISBN 9781788360074 paperback

A CIP catalogue record for this book is available from the
British Library and US Library of Congress

Jacket illustration: Philipp Foltz (1853) "Pericles Funeral Oration",
by courtesy of Stiftung Maximilianeum, München.

For if truth be at all within reach of human capacity, 'tis certain it must lie very deep and abstruse; and to hope we shall arrive at it without pains, must certainly be esteemed sufficiently vain and presumptuous.

— David Hume, A Treatise of Human Nature

Contents

Preface

In the eyes of the many, democracy has an aura of near sanctity. Government by the people, what could be of greater moral value than allowing people the freedom, the right to decide their own political fate.

Almost universally, democracy is seen as an, or even THE, ideal. It has become the standard of political legitimacy, based on a principle that is clear and simple. But the simplicity ends with that principle, as it has given rise to an uninterrupted stream of interpretations, definitions, political theories and philosophies — all pretending to catch its essence but with little agreement on what a political regime should entail to be labelled democratic.

At this point I cannot resist quoting that sharp observer of political life — I mean, of course, Sir Winston Churchill — who famously said, and I give you the complete quote: "Many forms of government have been tried before, and will be tried in this world of sin and woe. Nobody pretends democracy is perfect or all-wise. Indeed, it has been said that democracy is the worst form of government, except all those that have been tried from time to time."[1]

What I find remarkable is that Sir Winston Churchill refrains from defining democracy as an ideal, let alone THE ideal. But there seems to be a slight disappointment between the lines, unconsciously perhaps: is this the best we could come up with after hundreds of years of wrestling with the issue of what the best form of government should be?

It wasn't for a lack of trying though. Political theorists and philosophers have since time immemorial devoted great energy to developing systems of government to meet the highest standards. But this perennial debate had one particular feature that was—and still is—practically common to all political thought. Beginning with Plato and continuing through the centuries to modern times, theories have been overwhelmingly normative, i.e. on what-ought-to-be instead of what can realistically be done to achieve good governance. To coin and expression, I would call such theorizing as suffering from an "ought symdrome".

Thinking about the *res publica*, and about democracy in particular, should be firmly grounded in the terra firma of (political) reality, or lack relevance. The deep-seated weak–ness of most theories or philosophies is that they ignore what Raymond Aron has called *"l'inévitable imperfection de la nature humaine et de ses institutions"*. The irrationality and imperfection of the human mind cannot simply be swept aside.

"Ought" thinking strikes me as comparable to the work of an architect who designs a house, a bridge or whatever without knowledge of the properties of the materials he intends to use. His design may be beautiful, but the structure may collapse at an early stage if he misjudges the strengths and weaknesses of the material.

And the main material here, in *rebus politicis*, is Man. Human reality can't be moulded to suit a particular theory. "From the crooked timber of humanity nothing straight can be carved" (Kant).

A second, rather common, peculiarity of most political theorizing is what, in an ugly expression, I would call "illusional thinking". It is not just the normative thinking that often leads man astray, but also the confidence, the illusion that ideal solutions can be found.

"The concept of the perfect society is one of the oldest and most deeply pervasive elements in Western thought", says Isaiah Berlin.[2] In his introduction to his classic *Four Essays on Liberty*, he argues that it is mistaken that "this ancient and almost universal belief, on which so much traditional thought and action and philosophical doctrine rests, seems to me invalid, and at times to have led (and still to lead) to absurdities in theory and barbarous consequences in practice."[3] History provide ample proof to Berlin's thesis.

It is my intention to illustrate in what follows how man's imperfection coupled with "illusional thinking" more often than not leads to less than optimal results.

The "State", as an institution, a structure, might constitute an appropriate starting point for these reflections (Chapter I). The State is the skeleton on which a system of government—any system of government—is grafted. Without a state, no government. And no democracy, of course.

A next step (Chapter II) takes the argument to "Democracy" with a, perhaps biased, focus on its shortcomings, followed by a discourse (Chapter III) on the "Political Arena", the place where the action is and where the political battles are fought.

Democracy, as a human institution, will never attain perfection. In the "Conclusion", I venture to make a few suggestions on what could possibly mitigate some of the weaknesses.

The State

"If the state did not exist, would it be necessary to invent it?"[1] A somewhat surprising question perhaps, raised by Harvard philosopher Robert Nozick who was not above throwing the occasional stone in a quiet pond. It is, in fact, the opening sentence of his 1974 classic *Anarchy, State and Utopia*. For good measure he added on the next page: "The fundamental question of political philosophy, one that precedes questions about how the state should be organized, is whether there should be a state at all."[2]

A fundamental question indeed that has preoccupied philosophers since Plato. Thomas Hobbes, who preceded Nozick by some three hundred years, had a rather clear and unambiguous answer. *Homo homini lupus* — that was the crux. As he put it in his thundering prose: "Hereby it is manifest, that during the time men live without a common Power to keep them all in awe, they are in that condition which is called warre, and such warre is of every man against every man … In such conditions there is … no society; and which is worst of all, continual fear of danger and violent death. And the life of man, solitary, poore, nasty, brutish and short."[3] A common Power to keep them all in awe — and protect them, i.e. a state.

A view of man not shared, at all, by Jean-Jacques Rousseau who opened his *Du Contrat Social* (1762) with a proclamation of man's inborn innocence, corrupted only by society.[4] To be honest, I have to admit that I am not very fond of Rousseau. This has less to do with the fact that he was an egocentric and disagreeable fellow than with (my understanding of) his *Contrat Social*.[5] To my mind Rousseau got it wrong and Hobbes was much closer to the realities of an imperfect world. Where I part company with Hobbes, however, is that he, just as Jean-Jacques, has recourse to what is known as a social contract theory. I am walking on thin ice here but in my view it is unnecessary and erroneous to invoke any form of contract — not even hypothetical — between men[6] who one way or another have to live together. There has never been anything remotely resembling a "contract" in the sense of Hobbes, Rousseau, Locke, Kant, Rawls and countless others.[7]

The driving force that led man to develop bonds which ultimately resulted in the emergence of the "state" was the primordial quest for survival. Humans have, from the earliest times, formed groups, clans and tribes in order to survive. Anthropology, history and perhaps biology can teach us more about the origins of the state than the theoretical constructs of political thinkers. Individuals or tiny groups of individuals such as families had few means to survive in the "poor, nasty, brutish" world unless they were able to defend themselves. And obviously, the only way to get an adequate defence was to combine forces, to conclude alliances with other groups that had similar preoccupations. This was a natural process, nobody invented anything; at least at the beginning structures and institutions evolved gradually as needed. Groups grew larger by necessity as other groups grew larger as well, and many were often perceived as threats by others. Defensive systems began to develop as the new larger entities coveted the assets of weaker ones. Warre it was, and for ages it has been the way the world turns.

An author who, I think, well understood this process is Francis Fukuyama. I am not referring to his justly famous *The End of History and the Last Man*, but to his later book *The Origins of Political Order*.[8]

In this book he deals convincingly with the emergence of political institutions — and the state. Agreeing to a large extent with Fukuyama, and since he summarizes the position rather clearly, I can do no better than quoting him at length.

> Everything that modern biology and anthropology tells us about human nature … (is that) there was never a period in human evolution when human beings existed as isolated human individuals; the primate precursors of the human species had already developed extensive social, and indeed political skills; and the human brain is hardwired with faculties that

facilitate many forms of social cooperation. The state of nature may be characterized as a state of war, since violence was endemic, but violence was not perpetrated by individuals so much as by tightly bonded social groups. Human beings do not enter into society and political life as result of conscious, rational decision. Communal organization comes to them naturally, though the specific ways they cooperate are shaped by environment, ideas and culture.[9]

To add another voice to Fukuyama's, I note what Jesse Norman wrote in his excellent biography of Edmund Burke: "The social order is not, then, the result of any overall design. It is not the outcome of any specific plan or project. It evolves slowly over time. Different social orders may evolve in different ways, and some may be more effective and successful than others."[10]

In the end the political institutions as we know them now came into being. A defining moment was the emergence of a "centralized source of authority that held an effective monopoly of military power over a defined piece of territory".[11] In a similar way legal systems developed that turned ancient customs and traditions into written laws. The state began to get a structure which was further strengthened when rulers were forced to comply with the laws that held them accountable to bodies representing – segments of – the state's citizens. It led ultimately to our modern-day democracy.

But democracy, to be sure, was never a precondition for the emergence of a "state". States existed long before

Pericles's Athens. The ancient Egyptian kingdoms were states—so were the Mesopotamian, Indian and Chinese empires. States and empires rose, and "declined and fell", at all times and on all continents. Different as they were in many respects they all shared, in their heyday, one characteristic: they had a set of institutions that marked them as a state, an organized political community under a government. No state can hold together without a strong formal structure. No state can exist without a governing authority, a legal system, and the power to defend its territory. Democracy doesn't yet enter in the equation at this point. Let me get to it later.

- 2 -

Robert Nozick—a bit tongue-in-cheek, I suspect—may have questioned the necessity of a formally structured state, but in the end anarchy was not a solution for Nozick. He opted for a "minimal state limited to the narrow functions of protection against theft, fraud, enforcement of contracts, and so on ... and that any more extensive state will violate person's rights".[12] One who had no doubts whatsoever about the state was G.F. Hegel (1770–1831)—he would have been infuriated by Nozick. For him the question "whether there should be a state at all" would be absurd. The idea of a minimal state limited to the narrow function of protecting the individual would be sacrilegious. "The State", declared Hegel solemnly, "is the Divine Idea as it exists on earth. We must therefore worship the State as the manifestation of the Divine on earth ... The State is the march of God through the world ... The State is the actually existing moral life."[13] There is of course a moral law against quoting out-of-context, and Hegel's political philosophy is far more complex and profound to be dismissed on the basis of the above somewhat exalted quotations. Still, his conception of the state seems to be as removed as Nozick's, on the other end of the scale, from any workable ideas about what the state should actually be.

The point about Hegel, and countless others, is not only that they elevate the state to some unassailable moral height, but that they perceive the state — **The State!** — as something that has a value all of its own. It is not just more than the sum of its parts, the state is superior to that sum. It exists on its own, it has its own, independent, raison d'etre. It has intrinsic value. Not my view, for me the value of the state is instrumental, not intrinsic.

- 3 -

This brings me to a further point. The state, contrary to what Hegel may have suggested, is not a perfect institution. Not in its common everyday appearance, not even in its more "ideal" form. Intuitively, most people would probably agree, even without being very much aware why. Someone who did know exactly why was Nobel laureate (1986) James Buchanan. He was quite explicit, making it clear that he did not believe "... in the romantic delusion stemming from Hegelian idealism (that) the state was, somehow, a benevolent entity and those who made decisions on behalf of the state were guided by consideration of the general public interest".[14] I will come back to Buchanan later on.

At this point, when thinking about what form the state could take, I am somewhat led astray by Kant who was of the opinion that it is not really a problem: "… it can be solved (how crude it may sound) even by a people of devils (if they have any brain) … the clash of their conflicting opinions ('*Gesinnungen*') in a nation can be directed in such a way that they compel each other to place themselves under enforceable laws, leading to a state of peace in which laws prevail."[15] So, if even a bunch of mischievous devils can do it, a more reasonably inclined people should certainly be capable of over-coming "conflicting opinions", and develop an institutional structure that could, in the end, take the form of what we call a state. And they did. In the days of Ancient Greece Aristotle, who carried out a rather thorough research into the political organization of the Greek city-states, came up with more than 150 examples. Unfortunately, of his *Constitutions of States* only fragments have survived, although a complete text of the *Constitution of the Athenians* was discovered a century ago. In the *Politics* he describes, and analyses in more general terms, "The Classification of Constitutions" (Book III, Chapters 6–13) and the "Variations of the main types of Constitutions" (Book IV).

While the institutional framework can evidently take many forms, there is for me a basic underlying question.

And it is not "who should rule?" (Plato) or even "why should anyone obey anyone?" (Isaiah Berlin), but rather "how can we so organize political institutions that bad or incompetent rulers can be prevented from doing too much harm?" This was Karl Popper in his *The Open Society and Its Enemies*.[16] Popper acknowledged that John Stuart Mill had expressed similar ideas: Mill maintained that one had to assume that political power will be abused to promote the purposes of the holder and that laws and institutions should be designed to prevent such abuse.[17] I do agree with Popper, but I would add that it is not just the Hitlers, the Stalins or the Pol Pots of this world who do "too much harm". When they emerge from the dark the "clear and present danger" is obvious enough. But it is also the corrupt, the frauds, the swindlers, the criminal classes or just the ordinary cheats who are a menace, permanently on the look-out for weaknesses in the societal fabric that could be taken advantage of.

This is where I would signal a first clash—although one might consider it a minor one—between "Ought" and "Is". Most political thinkers, and political philosophers in particular, develop their theories about what the best institutional structure of the state should be on an assumption of man as a perfectly rational being, or perhaps not so much rational as "law-abiding"—at least if the laws have been adopted by due democratic process. Such theories fail to account for the problems, the dangers, deviants may create.[18] Surely, it is not possible to devise ideal structures that eliminate all possible causes of malfunction. Any theory that pretends to prescribe what form the state should take (the "Ought", par excellence) cannot afford to ignore Raymond Aron's admonition. This is what I meant by that "first clash". One cannot plausibly develop a normative theory on the subject (the "Ought" school) neglecting the imperfect "Is". This is where Popper's advice is so relevant. And it is for this very reason that all utopian and millenarian dreams so miserably fail. No human institution can ever be perfect by anyone's standard. Essentially, the question is—as Popper put it—how to limit potential damages. The separation of powers, a system of checks and balances, are fundamental in this respect. But of even greater importance is what is commonly called the Rule of Law—*l'Etat de Droit* or *Rechtsstaat* in respectively French and German terminology.

- 1 -

The Rule of Law means the primacy of the law, it means that the law is supreme—limiting the power of any institution that exercises political, or other, authority over the citizenry, whether executive, legislative or judicial.

The Rule of Law protects the people against arbitrariness and abuse of power by the state, as of right.[19] It provides the fundament for a society where individual freedom, personal autonomy and equality before the law prevail. In a state based on the Rule of Law citizens are able to act with a certain—never total, of course—confidence in the lawful behaviour of their fellow citizens and the public authorities. Without such trust in the predictability of the others' conduct social intercourse would be a hazardous affair. This, according to the economist Mancur Olson, is precisely the point: it is a necessary condition for a successful functioning of a market economy in as much as it guarantees the "secure and well-defined individual rights" of "all the participants in the economy, whether individuals or corporations, native or foreign, to the impartial enforcement of the contracts they choose to make".[20] The Rule of Law, moreover, ensures that "all participants have secure and precisely defined rights to private property … and defends (those rights) against other private parties and against the government as well."[21] The Rule of Law is undoubtedly the most fundamental of all requirements the well-organized society has to satisfy. Without it no community would be able to rise above a Hobbesian level of brute force and violence. Violence, the indiscriminate use of force, has no place in the well-organized society. Force should be exercised exclusively by the state, which should have what Max Weber has termed the monopoly of legitimate violence. The corollary here is—and I have the impression this is sometimes forgotten—that the state is to be held responsible for the physical safety of its citizens who are forbidden to take the law into their own hands. Security is primordial, a lack of security (whether real or only perceived) impedes the full exercise of liberty. No one feels free when threatened.

The importance of security is never contested when it is a case of "external threats". Protection against hostile military action is a top priority and no state can afford not to have the means to defend itself. "Internal security" gets generally a much lower priority, although internal threats pose a far greater and real danger to the citizens. If they do not have the right to defend themselves, then the state has the duty to ensure the safety of the population against any infringements whatever. A delicate issue here is that in order to guarantee safety the public authorities some-times have to limit freedom. This can go from relatively innocuous measures such as a curfew to quell public disorder to more controversial actions as the preventive detention of suspected terrorists, depriving them of their basic liberties. There are, I think, no hard and fast rules how to solve the issue. Neither liberty nor security are absolutes, and when they clash the only thing to do is to weigh carefully the pros and cons of any line of conduct, in the light of the particularities of the case in question. In the end, any decision is a matter of (subjective) judge-ment—ideally to be arrived at according to "the rules of the game".

Hardly satisfactory, I agree. But it is an illusion to think that clear cut answers are always available for all problems affecting man.

- 5 -

Popper's precept should include not only "bad and incompetent rulers" but the state itself and its various institutions as well. The state and its political and bureaucratic apparatus have an inbuilt tendency to expand. As if it suffered from some variant of Parkinson's law at work. Each individual or group that has some power within the state's realm seeks to enlarge its turf. This is entirely natural and in itself not necessarily a bad thing. Specific single bureaucratic or political decisions may be taken for unobjectionable or even praiseworthy motives, but in conjunction with other equally commendable decisions, an undesirable expansion of the government's territory may be the result. An autonomous growth that could become malignant, as increasing power leads to increasing loss of liberty and individual autonomy.

The state is empathically not the manifestation of the Divine on earth, it is even less the march of God through the world. This is what Buchanan has called – to quote him again – "a romantic delusion stemming from Hegelian idealism: the state was, somehow, a benevolent entity."[22] A romantic delusion indeed, leading to a belief that the state will always conform to some textbook model of optimal behaviour.[23]

What then can one reasonably expect from the state? I believe its role is, first and foremost, as Joseph Raz has put it, to promote and protect the interests of its subjects. Let me quote him in full:

> The only interest a government is entitled to pursue is the interest of its subjects. Talk of the interest of a government refers to is ability to pursue the interest of

its subjects in the way it ought to. It does not have an interest independent of, one which is not a reflection of, the interests of its subjects ... It is misleading to say that a government may, like anyone else, pursue its own interest within the bounds imposed by moral respect for the rights and interests of its subjects and of others. For the government's own interest is only what serves its ability to promote and protect the interests of its subjects.[24]

What these interests are is determined exclusively by the individual citizens, the subjects themselves. The state has no views, opinions or convictions of its own. The state does not think, does not feel — it is inanimate. It is neutral as to what is to be the "just" or "good" society. The state does not know ethics, does not have a normative philosophy. In fact, how can a group, a clan, a society have a separate conscience of its own? Isn't its "will" the aggregate of the "wills" — the choices — of its constituent members? Jean-Jacques' *Volonté Générale* (General Will) is a theoretical, abstract construct that may have helped him to come up with his *Contrat Social*, but it is an empty concept — in my irreverent view, of course.

Responsibility, accountability rests in the end with the individual, and with him alone. Roland Dumas, a former French Minister of Foreign Affairs, and a wily old fox, put it in this way:

> There is the ethics of the individual rooted in religion or in principle that I respect. But in politics there is no place for ethics. It is the raison d'état that prevails.[25]

Reinhold Niebuhr spoke of "Moral Man and Immoral Society", although perhaps "Amoral Society" would be more to the point.[26] The state has no authority to impose moral principles on its subjects. Rather it is there to make sure that the law is strictly adhered to.

But if it is to promote and protect the interests of its citizens the state does have a – positive – role to play as well. The precise content of that role is for the citizenry to decide, but whatever that role may be the state or more precisely the executive branch of the state should carry it out in the most efficient way and be held accountable for its actions. Ideally state action should be credible, predictable, transparent and consistent. Ideally … indeed. But the state (*pace* Hegel) and its institutions are run by eminently fallible humans. The important thing therefore is to limit possible harm to the maximum extent. And the first line of defence is a combination of the separation of powers, checks and balances, accountability of those in power and the Rule of Law.

A final observation: in the perception of many people the "state" is seen as a monolithic entity which can be a force to the good, as Hegel has it, or a potentially malevolent beast (Buchanan). In reality the state is however not an homogenous structure. It is a complex phenomenon composed of many parts and layers. Ideally these are kept in equilibrium by a system of checks and balances. Ideally that is, but in practice below the surface of the unitary state battles are continuously being fought between opposing political, economic and social interests.

This is of course entirely normal, only in an absolute dictatorship is the state a solid undifferentiated block.

A similar observation can be made with respect to the term "the people". Politicians in particular have a habit of referring to "the people", the desires and ambitions of which they invariably know how to interpret and which coincide, and not by chance, with their own. The problem here is that "the people" does not exist. Not as an indivisible ensemble of individuals with identical or even similar interests, ambitions and values. Of course, "a people" does exist. Many peoples exist, all made up of individuals who have much in common while at the same time may have different interests and values.

Democracy

-1-

Since Pericles, in 430 BC, delivered his famous Funeral Oration,[1] democracy as a system of government has practically monopolized the debate in political theory and practice.

But while it is generally acclaimed as the best regime, nobody contests that democracy has shortcomings, although not everybody agrees what they are. There are even those who are of the opinion that democracy is no good at all. They obviously include thinkers who are inclined to consider dictatorial regimes as the best system of government. They are in the distinguished company of Plato, who in *The Republic* makes a wonderfully scathing remark I can't resist quoting in full:

> Then in a democracy, I went on, there's no compulsion either to exercise authority if you are capable of it, or to submit to authority if you don't want to; you needn't fight if there is a war, or you can wage a war in peacetime if you don't like peace, and if there is a law that debars you from political or judicial office,

you will none the less take either if they come your way. It's a wonderfully pleasant way of carrying on in the short run, isn't it?[2]

Tongue-in-cheek perhaps, but the father of political philosophy certainly held no brief for democracy. Plato wasn't the only voice in Ancient Athens to reject democracy, there was Thucydides, for instance, who had no high regard for the *demos* which he referred to as the "mob". Aristotle as well had some problems with democracy as a political regime; he preferred a combination of oligarchy, aristocracy and democracy.

A second category does not reject democracy as conceptually mistaken, but warns against its inherent dangers—the major danger being a potential tyranny of the majority. Among its most prominent proponents one finds James Madison, Alexis de Tocqueville and John Stuart Mill. Their basic preoccupation is that unchecked majority rule could result in the suppression of the minority. As Albert Camus put it: "Democracy is not the law of the majority, but the protection of the minority."[3]

Then there are those who have no problem at all with democracy as a political regime, but who lament that it rarely in practice is functioning as it should. This is surely by far the largest group, and comprises most of those who write and think about politics. They all advance their particular reasons for the failure of democracy to live up to the theoretical ideal, but there is one overriding reason common to all. And that is the lack of involvement of the citizen, in Dutch often referred to as the gaping gulf ("*kloof*") between citizen and government. So, if a lack of involvement is the main problem then what would be more logical than to try and raise that involvement by having the citizens participate more fully in political life? Countless well-meant initiatives have been put forward — none of which had ever any significant, demonstrable effect on citizens' attitudes. Nevertheless there is, and there always will be, an unbroken succession of deserving attempts to persuade people to take an active part in public affairs.

Could it be that, somewhere hidden deep in the minds of many thinkers about political matters, there is an unrecognized nostalgia for the democratic practice of Ancient Athens where citizens actively participated in the political life of the *polis*? Athenian direct democracy would be the ideal, the standard against which all other political regimes should be measured. Perhaps. But while the Athenian citizens did take an active part in the running of their city, citizenship was a restricted category of adult males, totalling in the 4th century BC some 30,000, not more than a tenth of the whole population of Attica.[4] A low number indeed as Athenian citizenship excluded women, alien free-born residents (the so-called *metics*) and slaves.

Attractive as the idea of direct democracy might be, in our contemporary world it is not a practical proposition. Political entities are simply too large. What should not be ignored either in a nostalgic look back at Athenian democracy is the fact that the running of the ancient *polis* was considerably less complicated than that of present-day societies. The Athenian citizen who was involved in politics practically never had any "professional" qualifications. He was an amateur in the true sense of the word, and even selected by lot.[5] In addition one should note that he, while not always being a man of leisure, had a lot more time available to take part in political activities. The fact that most owned at least one slave made it all a bit easier.[6]

- 2 -

The issue of citizen involvement has, of course, raised a certain interest in academic circles, lifting the debate to a higher level of abstraction than customary in the deliberations of those with a more practical interest in the matter.

A good example of such a theoretical approach is the discourse about deliberative democracy.[7] In my view, most present-day democracies are deliberative anyway, but to meet the standards set in the academic debate much more is required than what is the going practice. And these standards are very strict indeed.

For a democratic decision to be legitimate it must be based on a number of principles. The most important concern the requirements that all relevant information is available to all, that all different points of view are taken into consideration and judged on the basis of their merits, that the debate is open to all and is conducted with civility and respect for different opinions. The avowed aim of the process would be to reach a consensus, not just a compromise, that is binding for all. This is a chimera, an illusion, particularly in the case of a "direct democracy": it is simply not feasible to involve an entire population in the deliberations—the vast majority will by necessity be left out. Anyway, the deliberations would be immensely time-consuming if justice is to be done to the proposed criteria. It is difficult to see how a government could function with efficacy at the national or even regional level. It may be a bit easier though in local matters, where the issues at stake are mostly less complex and where participants often have a direct interest in the matter at hand.

A representative democracy could come closer to the perceived ideal, but it would be too much to expect that the people's representatives will always conduct themselves in an exemplary, disinterested way. The opinions and interests of the parliamentarians often differ to such extent that decisions can only be reached by compromise —not the consensus the "deliberative democracy" so keenly paints as the ideal. Most theories of deliberative democracy seem to date from the nineties, but I have the impression that the earlier work of Jurgen Habermas was the inspiration for many, in particular *The Theory of Communicative Action*.[8] Habermas is surely one of the most prominent contemporary philosophers and his views on a large range of matters, including democracy, are widely respected.

One of the most fundamental questions regarding democracy is: how should the rules of the game, the democratic game, be arrived at and how do we ensure that they are legitimate? Habermas has given considerable thought to this.[9] For him, legitimacy rests on two premises: it must be based on autonomy of the citizens, and on cooperation and discussion between them in conditions of liberty and equality.[10] That is to say, first of all, Habermas does not look for any grounds or principles beyond, or external to, the human domain, such as natural law or some faith or belief. The source of authority, of power, is the people themselves, who are responsible for determining the principles and norms they have to adhere to. Very Kantian.

Secondly, legitimacy implies communication and dialogue or, as Habermas calls it, "discourse" or even "communicative action". Two premises that are rather appealing: individual liberty on the one hand, and the recognition that man does not live alone and has to accept his fellow human beings and their requirements on the other. Finlayson neatly summarizes Habermas's rules of the game: the voices of all should be listened to, no argument should be arbitrarily excluded from consideration, only the force of the better argument should prevail, which results in a consensus on the basis of reasons acceptable to all.[11]

In any case, democracy should be adversarial, not consensual. Striving for consensus means papering over real differences of objectives and interests that are part and parcel of any human society. Moreover, government needs dissent, an opposition to keep it alert and on its toes. Consensus, in the sense of a single political view, is undesirable as it risks being a first step to uniformity and worse beyond.

In this context, I would like to make another point. The various theories of deliberative democracy suffer from a weakness common to many tenets of political philosophy. The citizen is considered to be motivated purely and solely by reason. This is totally unrealistic. I will come back to this at length. Humans are, for a large part, driven by emotions, feelings, sentiments, instincts, desires (whether conscious or not) — in short, a range of influences and motives that are peculiar to the human mind. Any theory pretending to set norms for human conduct that overlooks this is lacking in rigour.

- 3 -

It is often argued that, short of direct democracy, the best method to involve the citizen in the political process is the referendum. The argument being that it puts the decision-making where it belongs, i.e. in the hands of the people. The referendum would seem nicely to solve the practical problems posed by a direct democracy, as it is on the one hand relatively easy to organize while at the same time it ensures the direct involvement of the people. These may be the advantages, but the disadvantages weigh heavier in the balance. In the first place, the outcome of the referendum can be influenced by the way the question is phrased. To give an hilarious example: Chilean voters were asked to answer yes or no to a proposition put to them in a referendum in 1978:

> In the face of international aggression unleashed against the fatherland, I support President Pinochet in his defence of the dignity of Chile.[12]

Secondly, some questions are too complex to be answered by a simple yes or no. Issues may need to be debated and the pros and cons sufficiently highlighted and weighed to arrive at a properly argued decision. Some 150 years ago already Walter Bagehot in his great work *The English Constitution* argued that population preferences need to be "filtered" through the institutions, of which Parliament first,[13] as these preferences are often based on irrational or plainly wrong assumptions. Thirdly, a more than occasional use of referenda may make it difficult for a government to pursue a coherent and consistent policy line. A too frequent use can even make a mess of government action, as shown by the experience of California, where the electorate regularly simultaneously opted for lower taxes and more spending for a specific purpose, such as e.g. roads or education or what have you. Fourthly, there is no one who can be held accountable for a decision taken by referendum. Well, the sovereign people of course, but that is not very helpful as there is no one in particular who has to suffer the political consequences. Fifthly, some argue that people lack the knowledge (to put it mildly) to decide on complex issues. This is of course an argument one has to be careful with — true as it may be. It sounds a bit insulting, but the point is rather that the lack of knowledge is caused not so much by stupidity as by the a lack of time. Voters simply do not have the time (or the ambition), as they had in Ancient Athens, to go into the many political issues modern-day society is faced with. Voters, I think, very well realize this and are content to leave the task to those specifically chosen for the purpose. Finally, the temptation to vote "No" in a referendum is for many hard to resist, it is a *pars-pro-toto* rejection of the government's policies without overthrowing it. This is particularly tempting when the proposal is very complex and a "No" vote will badly hurt the government. A case in point was the referendum on the EU Constitution. Whatever the merits of the proposal, some of the arguments advanced for a "No" vote often bordered on the ridiculous. Unhelpful of course was the fact that a large proportion of the electorate had not the faintest idea – or the wrong ideas – about what the proposed constitution actually contained. For instance, many thought the EU was to be given the authority to re-introduce compulsory military service.

- 4 -

This would seem to leave representative democracy as the only plausible alternative for the citizen to be involved in the governing of his *polis*. John Stuart Mill:

> The meaning of representative government is that the whole people, or some numerous portion of them, exercise, through deputies periodically elected by

themselves, the ultimate controlling power, which, in every constitution must reside somewhere. This ultimate power they must possess in all its completeness. They must be masters, whenever they please, of all the operations of government.[14]

The "deputies periodically elected" meant for some, notably Rousseau,[15] that these deputies or delegates receive instructions from their electors how to vote, they are not much more than a mouthpiece. Decisions are not theirs but the sovereign people's. Opposed to this delegate model, the "representation" model rejects the idea of binding instructions for the chosen, who as free agents can vote in accordance with their own conscience and opinions, and who have their own responsibility – for which they will be held accountable at the next election.

In his celebrated "Speech to the Electors at Bristol at the Conclusion of the Poll" in 1774, Edmund Burke set out the principles on which he would discharge his duties as the electors' representative:

> Certainly, Gentlemen, it ought to be the happiness and glory of a representative to live in the strictest union, the closest correspondence, and the most unreserved communication with his constituents. Their wishes ought to have great weight with him; their opinions high respect; their business unremitted attention ... But his unbiased opinion, his mature judgement, his enlightened conscience, he ought not to sacrifice to you, to any man, or to any set of new

living ... Your representative owes you not his industry only, but his judgement; and he betrays, instead of serving you, if he sacrifices it to your opinion.[16]

These are the principles of "representative democracy" which now is the system adopted by all democratic countries. It implies, in contrast with direct democracy, a certain distance between electors and elected. This is often seen as a shortcoming. I disagree, I see the distance as a good thing. I see it as a precondition for a workable parliamentary system. People have conflicting opinions and interests, and it is impossible to come up with actions that satisfy all and sundry. Compromises will have to be sought and Gordian knots cut, which is the parliamentarians' remit. They should of course not ignore "public opinion", but public opinion is not a homogeneous view shared by all. Parliamentarians should be wary of it. Oscar Wilde, always quotable, had a word of advice. In *A Woman of No Importance* Lord Illingworth, in reply to the question whether he regarded the House of Lords a better institution than the House of Commons, said: "A much better institution of course. We in the House of Lords are never in touch with public opinion. That makes us a civilized body."

Being civil is surely a commendable quality, but so is efficacy.[17] In order to function efficiently a representative democracy requires a good measure of independence. The need "to get on with it" is an undeniable necessity, especially in the complex contemporary world. This does not mean, needless to say, that the power of the parliament to make decisions should be beyond any control.

In a functioning democracy, the Rule of Law, separation of powers, checks and balances, transparency of the political process, accountability of those in power are all mitigating forces that help to limit damage—but they cannot eliminate it altogether. Perfection, absolute certainties are beyond the reach of man. We have to live not only with *"l'imperfection de la nature humaine"*, but also, as Aron added, the *"institutions sociales"*. To believe that mankind is, or will be, capable of solving its problems forever is an illusion, creating false hopes. Not for us the Millennium.

-5-

Curiously, the political class always blames the electorate for its low participation in the democratic process—which is considered almost indecent if not downright immoral. Voter cynicism and apathy, it is felt, are attitudes that badly need changing if untold disasters are to be avoided. It is the perpetual lament of all those who have a vital stake in the preservation of what they hold dear: the primacy of politics. Not just the politicians and their immediate circle, but also journalists and academics in related disciplines. The deplored cynicism and apathy of the voter, incidentally, is a fertile soil for analyses, learned papers, seminars, columns and newspaper articles— usefully contributing to the sustenance of those involved.

But are cynicism and apathy such bad things? A threat to democracy? The road to the abyss? Cynicism is, as *The Economist* calls it,[18] an intuitive suspicion of motives, an automatic discount of what politicians say and, particularly, what they promise. Cynicism in the sense of a critical attitude is, if anything, healthy. A lesson that history repeatedly has taught us. Apathy, a lack of interest in political matters, does not necessarily deserve condemnation either. It is a choice that every (non-)voter is at liberty to make, it is his right. A right that should be respected.

In Periclean Athens, though, participation in the political life was always regarded as of the highest value, people who didn't were called "*idiotes*". Aristotle considered man a *zoon politicon*, a political animal. But times have changed, life has become so much more complex that the range of matters demanding the individual's attention and energy has expanded immeasurably. Politics, for many, no longer has the priority that its *intimi* attribute to it. It is just one of the factors that influence life and well-being. Politicians have a tendency to ignore this. They assume that the citizens – the entire country – are interested in their activities. Of course they are right, to some extent. What politicians do and decide has relevance for the citizenry, but does the work of banks, the suppliers of energy, of food, of health services, of education ... etc.

The primacy of politics, as seen by politicians, is a notion fed to the population by the overriding attention it gets in the media. But the media are players in the same arena, so it is normal that they emphasize the importance of politics. It is their habitat as well.

That "gaping gulf" between politicians and citizens is a natural phenomenon and it is a misconception to think it has to be bridged. I believe the average citizen is not really all that interested in having a say in the political process, after all he has chosen representatives for the very purpose of solving the country's problems, without overly bothering him.

Let me add a further point. There is much ado about voters' "discontent", as if this is a recent deplorable tendency. I find this overdone. In the first place, discontent is not new but of all times. Secondly, it is perfectly normal. The differing demands of individual voters cannot be all realized simultaneously. For each there will always remain a gap between what is wished for and what is obtained. No one is ever entirely "content" with the outcome of the process. This can have a certain discouraging effect, resulting in a loss of interest in politics as an exercise over which the individual has little or no influence anyway.

All this is not to say, I hasten to add, that political apathy should be looked at with complete indifference. It is one thing to acknowledge an individual's right to "stay out of it", quite another to give free rein to those who profess to have a vocation to determine the destinies of a country as they think fit. The possibility "to throw the rascals out" should remain a constant and real threat to those in power. A threat that fairly regularly should turn into reality. To keep a democracy healthy a change of the guard is refreshing. Stagnant political waters inevitably begin at a certain moment to emit a strong offensive smell.

Democracy is not something static, as the French philosopher Frédéric Worms emphasizes.[19] It is what I call "a work in progress".

It is, moreover, not a goal in itself but rather a system of government that allows differing interests to work together in a competitive but peaceful matter. Without illusions to achieve perfection.

The Political Arena

Democracy, narrowly defined, is a system of government, a set of rules, procedures and institutional arrangements. It goes "live" when put into operation by human intervention — humans run the system.

All political thinkers have of course been fully aware of this fact and often have preceded their theoretical observations by commenting that any theory would have to take into account the constraints and idiosyncrasies of human nature.

There was, for instance, Spinoza who said in the Introduction to his *Political Treatise*:

> Therefore, on applying my mind to politics, I have resolved to demonstrate by a certain and undoubted course of argument, or to deduce from the very condition of human nature, not what is new and unheard of, but only such thing as agree best with practice ... I have laboured carefully, not to mock, lament or execrate, but to understand human actions; and to this end I have looked upon passions, such as

love, hatred, anger, envy, ambition, pity, and the
other perturbations of the mind, not in the light of
vices of human nature, but as properties ... pertinent
to it.[1]

And if this was not sufficiently clear, he admonished
theorists and philosophers or anyone concerned with
public affairs to conceive of men as they are and not "as
they themselves want them to be".[2] Spinoza, needless to
say, was not the only one to make the point. Machiavelli
peppered almost every page of *The Prince* with stern
warnings to "stick to the practical truth rather than to
fancies" (Chapter XV). There is even Rousseau — somewhat unexpectedly, I must say — who thought it essential
to "take men as they are" when developing theories
about "legitimate and sure government" (*The Social
Contract*, Book I). He did not, at least initially, under-
estimate the difficulties in understanding human nature,
though. In his *Discourse on the Origin of Inequality*, which
preceded *The Social Contract* by almost ten years, he had
already noted somewhat regretfully that "the most useful
and least advanced of all human sciences seems to me the
knowledge of man."[3] It still is, I fear. Yet underlying each
and every political philosophy or theory there is a
conception of human nature. This notion may be made
very explicit, as in the case of Machiavelli, or just
implicitly assumed without further argument or
explanation.

Explicit or implicit, these notions vary a great deal. At the risk of oversimplifying one could say that they range between two extremes:

- man is good by nature but corrupted by society,
- man is a nasty piece of work and needs to be kept in check.

The protagonist par excellence of the first view is Rousseau, with in his wake all those whose thinking contains a utopian streak. In the famous opening sentence of *The Social Contract* Rousseau proclaims his faith in the natural goodness of man: "Man was born free and everywhere he is in chains." If man is bad, it is not his fault but because society has made him so. I have always been puzzled by this. If man is good by nature, one must assume that all the individuals making up a group, a community, a society basically are good. How, then, does society corrupt them? Why should intrinsically good men derail once they are living together in a community? Is society something inherently different from the sum total of its constituent members? If that is the case, when and how does this radical alteration occur? Could it be that, perhaps, man is not entirely good by nature, but has a nasty streak that may come to the surface when in the company of others? Then there are those who are of the opinion that man not just has a nasty streak or two, but is nasty *tout court*. Machiavelli:

> For this can be said about the generality of men: that they are ungrateful, fickle, dissembling, anxious to

> flee danger and covetous of gain. So long as you
> promote their advantages they are all yours … When
> the need arises, however, they will turn against you.
> (*The Prince*, Chapter XVII)

In is later book the *Discourses*[4] — published in 1531 after
his death and by some considered as his political
testament — he was even more scathing:

> All writers on politics have pointed out, and through-
> out history there are plenty of examples which
> indicate, that in constituting and legislating for a
> commonwealth it must be taken for granted that all
> men are wicked and that they will always give vent to
> the malignity that is in their minds when opportunity
> offers.

For good measure he adds that "men never do good
unless necessity drives them to it; but when they are free
to choose and can do just as they please, confusion and
disorder become everywhere rampant."[5]

Somewhat more than a century later, Thomas Hobbes
wrote his classic *Leviathan*. Hobbes' thinking was
permeated by a profound lack of confidence in human
nature. Human beings needed to be kept strictly under
control if society was not to dissolve into chaos and
lawlessness. In the state of nature there would be no
safety for anyone as all are driven by "perpetuall and
restlesse desire of Power … (it being) manifest, that
during the time men live without a common Power to
keep them all in awe they are in a condition which is

called Warre; and such a warre, as is of every man against every man."[6]

He famously concludes that in the uncivilized, raw state of nature man had nothing to expect but a life that would be "solitary, poore, nasty, brutish and short".[7]

Between these two extremes of a fundamental goodness and a complete nastiness lies an infinite variety of views on "that dreadful universal thing called human nature" (Oscar Wilde). Each and every political thinker holds one, more often than not unconsciously, and most theories concerned with the "well-organized society" (Rawls) ignore the poor human beings that populate it. Why this is so, I fail to understand. Perhaps it would be interesting, as Erich Fromm suggested, to have a good look at "the character structure of the individual who creates a new doctrine and try to understand which traits in his personality are responsible for the particular direction of his thinking".[8]

Or, for that matter, take into account the context in which the author developed his theories. Hobbes, for instance, was much influenced by the chaos and ravages of the Civil War. Machiavelli was deeply involved in the intricacies of Florentine and Italian politics, while Rousseau … well, Rousseau was a complex character anyway.

As Gadamer has pointed out, individuals do not develop their ideas and theories in a vacuum but as members of a community, a society with its specific traditions, values and orientations.[9] Their thinking is rooted in their heritage and culture, which explains their inevitable "prejudices". Gadamer does not find this objectionable; on the contrary, someone has even characterized his philosophy as a "eulogy of prejudices"[10] in the sense of the shared conceptions and views originating in a common tradition and culture.

I think this is an insight that perhaps has not received the recognition it deserves. It strengthens the case of those who believe that in most of the social sciences—including political theory—objective truths are illusory. I love what Gadamer said to the philosopher Rudiger Safranski when asked to summarize his philosophy in a few words: "It could be that the other is right."[11] Sublime modesty, superb wisdom.

To return to the subject at hand, I do not think that one can say that man by nature is good or bad, nasty or noble. In each individual there are elements of goodness and badness. Sometimes the first trait is dominant, sometimes the second—each human being is a unique mixture of both. This seems to me a truth of such banality that it barely deserves stating. What is important, however, is to be aware of the potential for maliciousness that is lingering in the depths of each man's soul. It will not always, unavoidably, rise to the surface, far from it. But it is there, at least in some, waiting for a chance to strike when the risks of retribution are low enough. The laws of a "well-ordered society" are there to hold those risks at an appropriate level.

- 2 -

But there is another crucial matter that needs to be taken into consideration. The actions of man are not driven by reason alone. It would be unwise to base a political theory on the assumption that, since man is endowed with the ability to reason, he will do so to the detriment of all other possible drives.

Political behaviour — whether cooperative or antagonistic in nature — is, if anything, to a large extent determined by irrational motives. Sometimes these are benign, sometime malignant, but often strong enough to overwhelm reason. Isn't this the theme, par excellence, of great novelists?

The irrationality of man is a fact that cannot be argued away. But why, then, is it ignored in political theory?

My tentative explanation is based on the fact that political theory rose to eminence during the Enlightenment, a period when philosophy made short shrift of the old ways of thinking firmly grounded in the undisputable authority of King and Church. Inspired by the advances of modern physical sciences in the 17th century, the Enlightenment shifted the emphasis and stressed the power of independent thought no longer based on authority but on reason. Reason became the guiding principle of practically an entire body of political theory and philosophy.

It is only fairly recently that political theory stumbled on the fact that the human mind is not a cold and calm calculating machine when making decisions in political matters, objectively weighing pros and cons dispassionately. Non-rational forces and drives had for a long time been overlooked, and sometimes still are, in particular by social contractarians such as e.g. John Rawls. I am at a loss to understand why. It seems to me too obvious that man, in whatever he does or thinks, is influenced by a range of emotions, feelings, instincts, sympathies and antipathies, and so on.

In any case, the thinking has turned around. Perhaps due to Graham Wallas (1858–1932) who in 1908 published his *Human Nature in Politics*,[12] although I have the impression that his book was initially largely ignored.

In the introductory pages (not numbered) to the 1920 edition he makes his basic point:

> Political impulses are not merely intellectual influences from calculations of means and ends; but tendencies prior to, though modified by, the thought and experience of individual human beings. This may be seen if we watch the action in politics of such impulses as personal affection, fear, ridicule, the desire of property etc.

Whether Wallas was a forerunner or not of the change in thinking, it is striking that lately there has been a continuous stream of publications in the social sciences — notably economic and political theory — arguing that decisions are not taken on purely rational grounds. One could, for instance, mention Daniel Kahneman, the 2002 Nobel Prize winner who contested the rational model of decision-making.[13] Another author even unambiguously stated that "voter irrationality is the key to a realistic picture of democracy."[14]

Remarkably, Wallas has been given very little credit for his path-breaking work. Only Harold Lasswell referred to Wallas in his 1930 classic *Psychopathology and Politics*.[15] Lasswell himself is seldom mentioned either and merited only a fleeting reference in the *Oxford Handbook of Political Psychology*.[16]

Man may be a *zoon politikon*, as Aristotle said, but that does not mean he is rational political animal.

- 3 -

The first to perceive the relevance of Freud's clinical psychological methods for the analysis of political man was Harold D. Lasswell (1902–1978), a psychologist and Professor of Political Science at the University of Chicago, in the 1920s and 1930s a hotbed of excellence in the social sciences. Lasswell's *Psychopathology and Politics*, published in 1930, was a pioneering work of great originality albeit of a somewhat speculative nature. Lasswell himself was well aware of this and admitted as much in his Preface: "The first part of the book is in a rather dogmatic fashion, and this no doubt tends to obscure the highly unsatisfactory nature the materials and methods of contemporary psychopathology."[17]

And although Lasswell's in his own admission is not more than a multifaceted hypothesis not backed up by evidence, it seems to me to be a case of that plausible, intelligent insight that can provide a short-cut to an understanding that otherwise might not have been arrived at.

Lasswell's principal thesis, in short, is that political man "displaces" his private motives on to public objects and rationalizes this displacement in terms of (what he perceives to be) public interests.

In other words, the reasons given for a political action should not be taken at face value because the real motives are likely to have their origin in the unconscious substratum of the human psyche. They are obscure, not only to the outside world, but also to the individual himself. This, of course, applies not just to politicians. Lasswell:

> The political man shares ... the private motives, which are organized in the early life of the individual, with every man, and ... the displacement on to public objects, with some men. The distinctive mark of the homo politicus is the rationalization of the displacement in terms of public interests.[18]

Crudely put, a politician is fooling himself, and his voters, when he pretends to act first and foremost in the public interest. He rather seeks to satisfy his own, unconscious, personal needs of which he is largely ignorant. Political action, according to Lasswell, aims at self-aggrandizement, camouflaged as public spiritedness and greatly helped by a capacity to disguise self-interest as the pursuit of highly moral ends.[19]

What drives political man is an "emphatic demand for deference".[20] This "craving" for deference, as Lasswell calls it — or this need for self-esteem in Maslow's "Hierarchy of Values" — is of course not unique to the politician. It is shared by all men of ambition.[21]

One has to think only of CEOs of large companies whose demand for ridiculously high financial reward — what on earth is one to do with $50 or even $100 million a year — is not so much driven by greed as by reasons of prestige. To earn more than one's peers is the ambition, to prove oneself better than the others. But whereas your average chief executive wouldn't dream of pretending he is working to advance the public good, political man does. "Idealism is the noble toga that political gentlemen drape over their will to power", said Aldous Huxley.[22] An accusation of hypocrisy is perhaps unfair; it is more a question of vanity, I believe. Erich Fromm thinks that a high degree of narcissism is usual for politicians — he calls it an "occupational illness".[23]

In his novel *A Man in Full*, Tom Wolfe — who for some reason seems to have a special interest in vanities — paints a delightful picture of the phenomenon. The scene is set in the office of the Mayor of Atlanta, a black politician by the name of Wesley Dobbs Jordan.

Roger Black (who is white) comes to see the Mayor about some business that is of no further interest here. They come to talk about politics, which the Mayor admits he is hooked on.

"There is nothing else in the world like it."

And he continues:

"Do you know what politicians really love about politics—what makes politics so hard to give up once you've had a taste of it?"

Roger admits he doesn't know. Power, Fame, Money … he supposes.

"No," says Wesley, "… what really grabs you, what really turns you into a political junkie is … seein' them jump."

"Seeing them jump?"

"Exactly. Seein' em jump. Sometimes they're literally jumping up. Anytime I walk into a room, at least in Atlanta, everybody who's sitting down is going to jump up, even if it's the so-called business interests, which is our current euphemism for prominent white people. When it's time for me to sit down, somebody is going to jump to give me a chair. People in stores—not that I go shopping very often—they drop whatever else they're doing and jump to see to it that I have whatever I want … if I'm going to the airport to catch a flight, and I'm running late, they'll stop the whole damned airport to make sure I catch my flight, if that's what it takes, and if I'm walking through a public space, whether it's near City Hall or out at the airport or wherever, people—white people—will jump to get near me and coo the sweet things of fandom and ask for my autograph. Roger, that's what's addictive about politics: seein' em jump."[24]

The acerbic Jeremy Paxman devoted a highly readable book to the dissection of the soul of the politician: *The Political Animal: An Anatomy*.[25] Paxman, the journalist, comes to the same conclusion as Wolfe, the novelist: "In politics ... the prize on offer is significance. The desire for recognition, the acknowledgement by other humans of the worth of the individual."[26]

But where the novelist can bend and shape his fictive characters as he wishes, Paxman has the real thing. In a delightful chapter ("Getting In") he describes a day in the life of Boris Johnson, who at that time was campaigning as the Conservative candidate for Henley-on-Thames. Paxman and Boris Johnson — in his own equally readable and hilariously funny *Friends, Voters, Countrymen: Jottings on the Stump*[27] — describe the events of the day along similar lines.

Paxman, at that point in his story still in search of an answer to the question "why does anyone become a politician?", puts it to Boris who gives it an admirably honest answer. In his (Boris's) words:

> Why are you going into it, Boris?, says Jeremy as we trundle around the leafy lanes of Shiplake, ... Why am I doing it, Jeremy? I tell him: it's 30 percent a desire to be of public service or use, or however you want to express that with minimal piety. It is 40 percent sheer egomania; and it is 30 percent attributable to the belief that the world ought not to be run by swankpot journalists, showing off and kicking politicians around, when they haven't tried to do any better themselves, hmm, what, hmm?[28]

Johnson, I note, puts the egomania quota generously at 40 percent, where Paxman (p. 97) comes in at 30 percent only.

A last quote, from an ex-politician this time:

> MPs are a miscellaneous bunch, but united by this: a craving for applause. They are attention seekers. The job rarely offers real power or influence but regularly offers publicity. You may do little but you are somebody.[29]

The above anthology, I know, is rather limited in scope and the sources are all Anglo-Saxon. But a bit of further research would yield, I am sure, a good crop of quotable utterances from a worldwide range. Politicians have a lot in common, no doubt about it.

- **4** -

So much for vanity, pure and simple. It is easily recognizable and therefore perhaps no serious threat. There is, however, a variant of vanity that is less guileless as it hides itself behind a mask of moral rectitude — it is what I would like to call the Moral High Ground syndrome.

While politicians like Boris Johnson see no problem in admitting that they are "in it", at least partly, to satisfy their egomania, those suffering from the MHG syndrome pretend to higher motives (cf. Lasswell). What drives them are not base considerations of self-interest, but altruism, concern for others above all else. Their motives are unselfish, and vanity would be the last thing that animates them.

The urge to demonstrate one's principled purity in the pursuit of morally superior values is a powerful drive, especially when combined with the conviction that one is sacrificing one's own interest.

A former EU Commissioner, talking about his heavy workload once said: "I know I take risks with my health, but I am not complaining … I am so concerned about the well-being of others that I don't have the courage to think about myself. I don't love myself enough."[30]

No greater happiness than to be convinced of one's own virtue. Bernard Mandeville, the 18th-century satirist who delighted in ridiculing false pretenses, speaks of "… a Superlative Felicity which a Man, who is conscious of having performed a noble Action, enjoys in Self Love, whilst he is thinking of the Applause he expects of others."[31]

This tendency of many politicians to deceive themselves about what they are doing by invoking ethical or morally superior principles, or at least their good intentions, I find slightly risible.[32]

The MHG syndrome can also take the form of public ventilation of feelings of anger — and/or guilt — about the various kinds of injustice in the world. Moral indignation becomes a demonstration of one's integrity, which is deeply satisfying.

The most extreme form of the MHG syndrome is a lethal one: terrorism.[33] If there is one political philosophy (if one can call it that) where the end justifies the means, without exception, it is the belief of the terrorist that the world can only be saved by destroying it.

It is based on the conviction that society, and in particular capitalist society, is so desperately ill that only radical, immediate and ruthless surgery can redeem it. Only revolution can lead to a perfect society, gradual evolution is impossible, so it must be destroyed and rebuilt from the bottom up. Only an "armed struggle" can annihilate injustice and liberate the "oppressed masses". Utopia is not The Impossible Dream, but the Promised Land to which the revolutionary vanguard will lead the trampled-on proletariat. To get there nothing will be allowed to stand in the way.

The peculiarity of the mental make-up of the political terrorist is that he can leave no room for dialogue. His convictions are absolute, based on two unshakeable pillars: the moral superiority of the end he is fighting for, and the objective, scientific truths of Marxism, or his own particular theories underlying his political analysis. A typical example, by way of illustration: Pierre Carette, the leader of the Belgian terrorist group "Cellules Communistes Combattantes", received a life sentence for his part in a bombing campaign (1984–1985) against banks, political parties, American business interests and military targets. At his (conditional) liberation in 2003, after a total of 17 years in prison, he declared in an interview:

> It is more evident than ever: mankind will never
> overcome barbarous capitalism unless the
> imperialistic bourgeoisie is eliminated. The future has
> only one name: communism ... Only violence can
> overthrow the bourgeois ... Revolutionaries have a
> duty to bring to an end the abuses and crimes of
> capitalism They have to fight for that, of course that
> means violence.[34]

This more than conviction, more than belief. This is
dogma, a rigid logic impervious to dialogue or counter-
argument. While all messianic terrorist groups claim that
their revolution will bring the perfect society, none of
them actually gave any indication as to what that society
would look like.[35] In this they were good disciples of
Marx, who didn't either.

The Italian Brigate rosse, for instance, were quite
loquacious, producing an endless stream of pamphlets
full of the long-winded verbiage that is a trademark of
Marxists the world over. But nowhere—in none of their
documents, communiqués or *"volantini"* —was there ever
any explanation of what they envisaged for post-
revolutionary Italy.[36] They seemed to operate under the
illusion that once the revolution had been successfully
completed *"tout sera pour le mieux dans le meilleur des
mondes possible."* A (bloody) fairy tale with a happy
ending—in spite of the historical evidence to the contrary.

But there are others who struggle as well, less
belligerently though, for space on the Moral High
Ground, always in danger of overcrowding. They are the

ones who proudly march from the lowlands of everyday life towards the hills where, as the chosen, they will ascend to the pristine alpine pastures and there bask in the sun of moral virtue. They carry banners in all colours of the rainbow exhorting people to be nice to each other and not invade other countries. On their way up they notice along the road the uncomprehending bystanders who so evidently are lacking in righteousness, solidarity, idealism, humanism, environmental concern, multi-cultural awareness, anger about third world poverty, indignation about injustice, and moral principles in general.

I cannot but envy them their certainties, their feelings of moral superiority, their principled stand on every great issue of the day, their conception of politics as a series of great moral occasions to lend one's voice to a protest,[37] their intolerance for any opinion other than their own. I suppose they probably have never heard of wise, old Gadamer who warned us: "It could be the other is right."

Leaving the Moral High Ground behind I want to turn to another, less lofty subject: power. Many see a lust for power as the prime motivation of political man. Whether this is always the case is debatable, but the "craving for deference" can smoothly glide into a craving for power – and so force the manifestations of deference by others. Moreover, it easily results in feelings of superiority, often as a compensation for an inferiority complex (Adler, Jung et alii). Power, then, is not a means towards an end, it is an end in itself.[38]

The exercise of power is deeply satisfying, it gives prestige and even increases the sex drive. As Henry Kissinger, who should know, observed: "Power is the ultimate aphrodisiac."[39]

Whether its drives originating in the dark unconscious are cravings for status, a need to dominate others because of an inability to dominate oneself, or a desire for material wealth, an instinct for aggression, resentment, a deeply seated inferiority complex, or carnal lust—they are all manifestations of self-centredness. Power is sought for selfish motives[40] and, in the interest of all, needs to be controlled. Lord Acton's is a warning to heed at all times.

Power can even have an intoxicating effect on leading politicians—and on leaders in other fields as well, of course—affecting their actions and decisions in dangerous ways. Lord Owen, a former UK foreign minister (1977–1979) and a trained physician and psychiatrist, has analysed how power can lead to excessive self-confidence, overestimation of competence and contempt for the advice and opinions of others when that goes against what they themselves think. This often results in hubristic behaviour and disastrous leadership.[41]

However dangerous power in the wrong hands may be, it is clear though that no society can function without a locus of power or authority—without leadership in other words.

It applies not only to forms of political association, but just as well to any other type of organization, be they businesses, trade unions, the Church, the Army (!), sports clubs … For all, leadership is an indisputable requirement, a fact of (organized) life. Leadership is the bond, the force that holds it all together, without it there would be disorder, instability and confusion.

If one accepts the need for leadership—and only anarchists would not—then it follows almost mathematically that leadership is exercised by a few, the "chosen few "literally in a democracy. Leadership by the many is a *contradictio in terminis*.

- 5 -

What does it take to be a successful politician? The question has fascinated political thinkers from the earliest times, from Hammurabi onwards to the present day. An avalanche of recommendations, prescriptions and requirements about the desired qualities, virtues and capabilities has cascaded down through the centuries—as well as an equally long list concerning undesirable particularities.

Ideally a politician should be wise, righteous, courageous, reliable, dignified, unpretentious, humane, generous. He should certainly not be dishonest, egoistic, shifty, ambitious, vain and, in general, not have the opposite of any of the positive character traits above. A personification of human perfection in other words. Not on offer in this imperfect world.

Some have drawn up lists of "dos and don'ts" to help aspiring politicians to climb the ladder. A particularly shrewd one was Cardinal Mazarin (1602–1661), the

Italian-born naturalized Frenchman (in 1639) who from 1642 until his death effectively ruled the country under Louis XIV. His *Bréviaire des Politiciens* — a manual for politicians — is a mine of clever and lucid advice, totally amoral as Mazarin only cared about efficacy and did not show the slightest interest in ethical considerations. The *Bréviaire* consists of more than fifty short chapters, each dealing with a single subject without an immediately apparent connection between them. It is more an anthology of maxims than a structured discourse. Mazarin covers a vast field indeed, from the correct appearance to the importance of hiding one's feelings. Always act with prudence and avoid being caught unawares.

"Know yourself," says Mazarin (remembering Delphi), "know your adversaries, their weaknesses and strengths, simulate and dissimulate, don't trust anyone, always speak well of others but think before you speak."[42]

All very down-to-earth, with the sole aim to outsmart the other by whatever (legal) means. Recommended reading for today's politicians. More principled advice for parliamentarians was given by Edmund Burke (1729–1797). In his famous speech to the electors of Bristol (1774) he argues that a Member of Parliament should always follow his own judgement when voting and not just do what his electors tell him.

Politicians may differ in many respects but they have all, without exception, one thing in common: their most important tool is the word. For this we have to thank – or blame, if you wish – the Ancient Greeks or, more precisely, democratic Athens.[43]

People have been discussing and arguing about questions regarding their communal life since time immemorial, but not since the Athenian *polis* did this take the form of an organized, structured debate. Issues were decided not by force but by persuasion. Eloquence, *"Retoria"* in Greek, the ability to speak cogently and convincingly was a requisite for any politician wanting to have influence and authority in the Assembly where decisions were taken by vote. Speech became the tool of politics par excellence forever since. "Politics", observed Dutch politician Frits Bolkestein, "is 90% rhetoric."[44]

In this context it is not without interest to note that the *Concise Oxford Dictionary* gives two slightly differing definitions of rhetoric:

- the art of effective and persuasive speaking or writing, and
- language designed to persuade or impress (often with an implication of insincerity or exaggeration).

The politician lives by the word. It is not only the tool of his trade, it is also his "product". Words are what he produces and sells. The product takes the form of speeches, statements in the media, party programmes, resolutions and motions in political assemblies, and – most important of all – laws. With the delivery of the speech, the formulation of the statement, the adoption of the motion or the law, the politician's job basically is done. The task of turning the words into deeds is for others.

Political language has become an art form in itself. The jargon can be entirely incomprehensible if not misleading. George Orwell pushed this to its absurd extreme with his Newspeak.

But political rhetoric can also rise to great heights, as illustrated by Simon Hoggart's hilarious report of a speech by Tony Blair.

> Not for the first time, I was struck by the way that a Blair speech is closer to a musical composition than to mere rhetoric. Like a piece of music, its aim isn't to inform but to create feelings. It's no more about facts and politics than the Pastoral Symphony is an examination of the Common Agricultural Policy. And like a piece of music, it has a definite structure, based on rhythm and repetition. A theme is introduced and merged with the earlier ones. The repetition brings a satisfying familiarity so that by the end the listener's brain vibrates with all the interwoven passages.[45]

The speechifying can easily become an ingrained habit, difficult to shake off even when clearly inappropriate such as when Queen Victoria complained of Gladstone: "He speaks to me as if I were a public meeting."

As battles in the political arena are fought with words as weapons, the politician needs to hone his verbal skills. He will get nowhere without a well-developed "gift of the gab" which my *Concise Oxford Dictionary* elegantly defines as "the facility of speaking eloquently or profusely" observing that, colloquially, gab means "chatter, twaddle".

The clear and present danger is that words are free: there is no charge and the supply is unlimited. This can lead to an overdose. The temptation, hard to resist, is to outbid the opponent – in the Schumpeterian competition for votes – by making promises that cannot possibly be kept. The result is a lack of credibility of politicians' utterances and, consequently, a low confidence in the political process. Invariably, politicians top the list of any opinion poll ranking professional categories as to unreliability, with the media – manipulators of words as well – in an honourable second place.

As John Dunn, Professor of Political Theory at Cambridge, put it with a nice turn of phrase, "… politics has come to be a vaguely degrading and highly specialized occupation … plainly a career wide open to all but unmentionable talents and an occupation totally unfit for gentlemen – let alone gentlewomen …"[46]

Politicians are, in general, disliked, vilified and blamed for everything that goes wrong. Nothing new here: "*Gubernatorum vituperatio populo placet*", the Romans observed ("to speak ill of the rulers pleases the people").

For this they have themselves to blame. Not just by making untenable promises, but also by the level of the political debate. It is often difficult to take serious the quarreling by politicians in the different parliaments, in the written media, on TV talk shows.

The opposition has the right to oppose, surely. It is even its duty to scrutinize critically the government's every step. But it is not credible when every single proposal of the other side is dismissed as wrong, stupid or—when agreed with—as something that has been proposed "by us" long ago. The others are always mistaken ... our side has always been right.

I remember with affection Georges Marchais, the late French Communist leader, who was the undisputed champion of this line of argument.

- 6 -

More than competition, as Schumpeter argued, politics is a battle. Sometimes fought fairly and squarely according to generally accepted rules, and sometimes with little or no regard for rules. But always a battle.

At stake: power, the ability to impose one's own priorities. Human ends and purposes necessarily differ and politics is the scene where the conflicts are fought out. This has little to do with ethics, with virtue, with notions of Good and Bad. "I have never regarded politics as the arena of morals. It is the arena of interests", said the British Labour politician Aneurin Bevan (1897–1960) once. James Buchanan thought along similar lines: "Politicians in elected offices seek re-election, and this dictates that they be responsive to the desires of constituents. And constituents seek to profit from politics just as they seek to profit from their private activities."[47]

Politics, as a process, a method, is ethically neutral. It takes place, not on the Moral High Ground, but on the amoral low ground. Where, as Aron says, "a good policy is defined by its efficacy, not by its virtue."[48] To claim otherwise reeks of the vision thing, the whiff of righteousness that suggests higher values. As has often been observed, Hitler, Stalin, Pol Pot et alii had a vision. Utopists have a vision. Robespierre had one.

To have a grand vision is one thing, to contribute "*avec efficacité*" to the functioning of democratic society another. That is not to dismiss all visionaries as potential Pol Pots. They may be, and undoubtedly they often are, highly principled, but then theirs is what Max Weber called a "*Gesinnungsethik*", the ethics of good intentions with small regard for the ultimate outcome.

There is however a vision—perhaps it is better to speak of an opinion or a "vision-light"—that is shared by the entire political class, and all who gravitate around it: it is the "Primacy of Politics".

It would of course be absurd to deny the importance of politics and the political process, but to proclaim the "primacy of politics" is overdone. It creates the impression that politics ranks above all other forms of human interaction. As if it were an end in itself to which all else is subordinated. As if a political ideology could be equated with a faith, a religion. Reading the newspapers, watching the news on TV, etc. may, anyway, give an exaggerated view of the role of politics in the life of the citizen. Politics is not as all-determining as politicians and their coterie of opinion makers want us to believe. Increasingly, societal processes unroll outside the confines of the political arena. This is not, in itself, a bad thing: a major task of politics is "to remove obstacles to the exercise of individual choice rather than lots of fussy interventions on our behalf".[49] A bit hard to swallow perhaps for those of interventionist convictions, moreover no politician of whatever colour is pleased by a down-grade of his possible exercise of power.

Primacy of politics, or primacy of politicians then … ? Anyway, the real primacy should be the primacy of the law.

Politics, rather than a vocation or a calling, now is a full-time career, and thus, logically, the principal aim of those who have chosen this profession is to advance that career. It must therefore be a natural inclination to try and enlarge the theatre of operations rather than restrict it, and so broaden the range of opportunities for a rise on the ladder. It is, for instance, far more tempting to vote for an increase in public spending than to cut public expenditures and so create an aura of benevolence and caring. Tempting especially since the money is not one's own.

-7-

Democracy is—I repeat—competition. It is a contest between personalities, interests, values, ideologies. Raymond Aron: "I think one could define democracy, in sociological terms, as the organization of a pacific competition to achieve power."[50]

"Pacific" is the key word. In a democracy differences are reconciled, conflicts resolved by "pacific competition", i.e. without recourse to force. Competition is a healthy phenomenon in *rebus politicis*. It was Machiavelli who was, I believe, the first to make the point in the *Discourses*. The title of Book I.4 reads "That Discord between the Plebs and the Senate of Rome made this Republic both Free and Powerful", which he elaborates as follows:

> To me those who condemn the quarrels between the nobles and the plebs, seem to be cavilling at the very things that were the primary cause of Rome's retaining her freedom, and that they pay more attention to the noise and clamour resulting from such commotions than to what resulted from them, i.e. to the good effects which they produced. Nor do they realize that in every republic there are two different dispositions, that of the populace and that of the upper class and that all legislation favourable to liberty is brought about by the clash between them.[51]

The strong point of a healthy competition is that it is a dynamic, driving force. It stimulates people to do better — better than before and better than others. It is a source of progress and inventiveness.

Carl Jung also valued the competitive element: "True democracy is a highly psychological institution which takes account of human nature as it is and makes allowances for the necessity of conflict within its own rational boundaries."[52]

To me it is no less than a mystery why the vast majority of political theorists have ignored the obvious. Democracy cannot, in real life, be anything else than a contest. A pacific one perhaps (Aron), but a contest, a battle all the same.

They were principally concerned with what in their opinion democracy "should be" — firmly in the Ought camp — sidestepping that awkward impediment to the elegant coherence of their theory: human nature. I know I keep coming back to this ad nauseam, but it is my firm view that there is no place for a theory that ignores the imperfectability of whatever is human — human nature, human institutions, human thought processes, etc. To pretend the opposite is utopian, but more importantly it is dangerous.

Of course not all political thinkers can be tainted with this same brush. There is, for instance, John Dunn:

> Politics is the balance of conflict and cooperation between human purposes on any scale on which you care to look at it … Human purposes are very heterogeneous … Likewise human judgements … in a human world increasingly dominated by the search for personal profit and monetary advantage the chances of human purposes and judgements converging on clear and convincingly public goods and shared preferences are very slight.[53]

I also like what the young Dutch philosopher Luuk van Middelaar wrote:

> This utopia of a rational, post-political harmony rests on the point-blank denial of the impossibility to put an end to the social conflict that lies at the basis of human society.[54]

It was the political philosopher Chantal Mouffe who came up with a theoretical underpinning for an adversarial rather than a consensual form of democracy.[55] She believes that such thinkers as Rawls and Habermas are on the wrong track. The "deliberative democracy" which they so ardently promote rests on a fundamental misunderstanding of human sociability. They neglect the "antagonistic dimension constitutive of the political".[56] The adversarial character of real-life democracy is, as I have argued earlier, a healthy phenomenon that, more-over, cannot be reasoned away. Mouffe therefore sensibly proposes that:

> Instead of trying to design the institutions which, through supposedly "impartial" procedures, would reconcile all conflicting interests and values, the task for democratic theorists and politicians should be to envisage the creation of a vibrant "agonistic" public sphere of contestation where different hegemonic political projects can be confronted. This is, in my view, the sine qua non for an effective exercise of democracy.[57]

A few pages further she defines what she means by agonism:

> This is the type of relation which I have proposed to call agonism ... agonism is a we/they relation where the conflicting parties, although acknowledging that there is no rational solution to their conflict, nevertheless recognize the legitimacy of their opponents. They are adversaries not enemies.[58]

Mouffe has no problem admitting that she has been inspired by the work of Carl Schmitt (1888–1985), a controversial thinker to say the least, whose views ultimately led to a defence of Hitler's dictatorship.

This was of course not what Mouffe had in mind, it was rather Schmitt's thesis that "the specific political distinction to which political actions and motives can be reduced is that between friend and enemy."[59] But where for Schmitt the friend/enemy distinction implies "antagonism", which can lead to a destructive conflict, for Mouffe the relationship is not between enemies but adversaries, which she calls "agonistic". An adversary being "somebody whose ideas we combat but whose right to defend those ideas we do not put into question".[60] This, I think, is the correct approach when one seeks to develop a coherent and relevant theory of democracy.

Such theory should, moreover, be multidisciplinary, taking in insights from psychology, anthropology, sociology, economics and philosophy of course — in fact from the broad scale of the social sciences.

As could be expected Mouffe came under attack. Her critics, academic and other, mostly missed the point, however. Mouffe develops her theory from what I call the "Is" angle, whereas her opponents invariably start from the "Ought" position. Normative political theory clearly is still the flavour of the day. None of its proponents shows any concern whether their normative prescriptions could ever be translated into political reality. Which is of course the point — in fact, the one and only point.[61]

In the political arena it is not so much the run-of-the-mill politicians who are the major cause for concern. It is those who are looking for the weak spots of the system who do the damage. They come in varying degrees of mischief, ranging from the totally corrupt to those who commit silly offences, such as having a duck pond installed at taxpayers' expense. It is an illusion to think that political misdemeanour can be eliminated, just as all other forms of misdemeanour.

The only thing to do is, in Karl Popper's words, to try and organize political institutions so that bad or incompetent rulers can be prevented from doing too much harm.

A few words about that in the concluding chapter.

Conclusion
The Argument Revisited

- 1 -

Democracy being a human institution is, as I have been arguing unremittingly, not perfect. It is, one might say, inherently unstable, it even carries within itself the seeds of its own destruction convincingly demonstrated by Hitler's Nazi party's perfectly regular electoral victory in 1933.

Such complete breakdown, fortunately, is rare, exceptional even. But democracy hides other potential dangers in its bosom. As pointed out by John Stuart Mill and Tocqueville among others, it can lead to a "tyranny of the majority".

A rare occurrence of course but other flaws are evident in even the most democratic of countries. If one accepts the principle that each citizen has a vote and that each vote has equal weight, then both the USA and the United Kingdom fall short of this lofty principle.[1]

Democracy's "openness" as a system of government is undoubtedly its strength. It is unique in the sense that it allows space to differing political convictions, beliefs, ideologies and values.

But at the same time this openness is also its principal weakness. Democracy has no "built-in" defences. More than any other political regime it is vulnerable to negative forces that seek to take advantage of this openness, and in the most extreme case even to destroy it. To be able to function properly, democracy needs to be shored up by surrounding it with protective defensive walls. These include, as mentioned in Chapter II, the separation of powers, checks and balances, the Rule of Law and so on. These defences are not inherent characteristics of a democracy. They have to be added on to it. Which of course does not always happen—unfortunately.

- 2 -

In fact I see little ground for optimistic views about mankind's moving toward an ideal world. Wishful thinking is not helpful, it is a road to nowhere.

Does this mean then that we are left standing helplessly outside, drenched in the cold rain of sombre pessimism? Paradoxically, we would be indeed if we were to rely on what John Gray has called the "prozac of the belief in progress", the belief in "that long march towards what will be heaven on earth".

But even if that heaven will remain out of reach, it does not mean that man is necessarily left without any possibility to improve his lot. Not by any radical methods though, but in a typically human way by tentative steps, not always going in the right direction, but advancing nevertheless by trial and error. It is what Karl Popper has called the method of "piecemeal engineering".[2]

Karl Popper (1902–1994) was a many-sided man. His initial claim to fame was as a philosopher of science, his work on logic and the scientific method has been widely praised. But he also took a keen interest in political theory—and practice—and was a passionate defender of liberal values. This passion is particularly evident in *The Open Society and Its Enemies* (1945) where he attacks the principal proponents of the "closed society", as he calls it, i.e. Plato, Hegel and Marx.[3] His purpose was to destroy the foundations of all authoritarian politics and deterministic philosophies which he dismissed as pseudoscience. He did not mince his words and his violent attacks on three icons of philosophy did nothing for his popularity in polite academic society. Plato was accused of totalitarianism, racialism and tribalism. He betrayed Socrates and "compromised his integrity with every step he took".[4] In passing, Aristotle gets told off for "at times elaborately and solemnly missing the point" as well as "lacking historical insight".[5] But Popper reserves his main contempt for Hegel who is doused with vitriol by the bucket load. The reader is warned against "Hegel's bombastic and mystifying cant" and "this gibberish from Hegel's Philosophy of Nature".[6] ... "I do not even think he was talented," fumes Popper, "he is an indigestible writer ... Supreme only in his lack of originality."[7] With great relish he then quotes Schopenhauer, who considered Hegel as "a flat-headed, insipid, nauseating, illiterate charlatan who reached the pinnacle of audacity in scribbling together and dishing up the craziest nonsense".[8] Only for Marx did Popper have a certain respect. He admired his "openmindedness, his sense of facts, his distrust of verbiage ... His sincerity in the search for the truth and his intellectual honesty distinguish him (as) one of the most influential fighters against hypocrisy and pharisaism."[9] But Popper was very critical as well: "Marx was, I believe, a false prophet ... responsible for the devastating influence of the historicist method of thought within the ranks of those who wish to advance the cause of the open society."[10] Whatever one may Popper accuse of, he certainly had the courage of his convictions. No dilly-dallying for him. But all this, entertaining as it might be, is beside the point, i.e. the main point Popper wants to make.

In Chapter 9 of the first volume of *The Open Society and Its Enemies*, which deals with Plato, Popper states that in his view Plato's way of treating politics is dangerous. "The Platonic approach I have in mind can be described as that of Utopian engineering, as opposed to another kind of social engineering which I consider as the only rational one, and which may be described by the name of piecemeal engineering."[11] The utopian approach determines, at the outset, the "ultimate political aim, or the Ideal State, before taking any practical action".[12] Once this ultimate aim has been decided upon a blueprint of the Ideal State can be drawn up and a plan for action formulated. Utopian engineering implies (re-)designing society as a whole from the ground up. What Plato himself called wiping "the slate of human society and human habits clean", (starting with) a clean canvas.[13] It is a typically holistic approach allowing no deviations from the set path to the Ideal State, the one absolute and unchanging aim. It demands strong leadership and centralized rule by a small elite minority. Ultimately, it is likely to result in dictatorship.[14]

Piecemeal social engineering, on the other hand, is more modest in its aims, and instead of adopting a rigid all-embracing approach, it proceeds by small steps. It seeks improvements through "piecemeal social experiments ... carried out under realistic conditions in the midst of society".[15] It recognizes that social institutions are best not purposely designed, but should grow and develop naturally. It is a continuing process of reforms, improvements and corrections, guided by pragmatic and critical considerations that have no truck with messianic final solutions. It is based on the understanding that in order to make progress man must be allowed to make mistakes — it is a method of trial and error. The antithesis of utopianism, that greatest of political delusions.

Contrary to utopian engineering the step-by-step approach does not carry much risk of upheaval, of revolutions or violence. It can deal with the quirks and idiosyncracies of man, the need for checks and balances, and it perfectly suits a democratic decision-making process.

Its advantages are undeniable, but what it is said to lack—and for its opponents this is too good a chance to miss—is "vision", a broad, sweeping high-minded view of man's destiny. Piecemeal engineering is not glamorous, it is pedestrian and a bit messy. It is much more gratifying, intellectually and morally, to develop Grand Ideas that deal with the "should" and ignore the "could". No place as meritorious as the cathedra of the Moral High Ground.

History has amply demonstrated that any form of utopian engineering has been a failure, not infrequently leading to terrible disasters. Piecemeal engineering, I insist, is the only sensible way.

The merit for this idea is not exclusively Popper's, though. He was preceded by a few others of whom he may not have been aware—at least I found no references to any of them in his writings. But credit where credit is due and that is first of all the Emperor Marcus Aurelius (AD 121–180), the last of the Five Good Emperors and an independent stoic philosopher as well. He wrote a series of observations and reflections not meant for publication but "To Himself", as he said. They were later published anyway and are known as the *Meditations*. This is what Popper missed:

> Don't hope for Plato's republic; but be content with the smallest steps forward, and regard even that result as no mean achievement.[16]

It is also interesting to note what Tocqueville had to say on the subject:

Shouldn't we consider the gradual development of the institutions and the democratic customs not as the best, but as the only means to remain free?[17]

- 3 -

If one accepts — reluctantly, even — "*l'inévitable imperfection*" of democracy, what can one realistically expect of it as a system of government? Or, to approach the matter from another angle, assuming that democracy advances by trial-and-error, step-by-step (Popper's piecemeal engineering), what are the major threats and what can be done to mitigate potential dangers?

The answer to the first question is, I fear, disappointingly simple: it all depends. It depends on the particular circumstances of the particular case, the state a particular political entity — a country, say — finds itself in. There is no pat answer.

Democracy can work very well when conditions are optimal. That means, I repeat myself once again, a strong state with stable institutions, free and fair elections, Rule of Law, separation of powers, checks and balances, transparency of the political process, accountability of those occupying the seats of power and a respect of fundamental freedoms such as the freedom of thought, of expression, of association and assembly.

A tall order indeed, and it is rare that these conditions are fulfilled simultaneously. In most countries that claim for themselves the epithet "democratic" one or more conditions are, in practice, not entirely complied with or, perhaps less often, not at all. One may recall, for instance, the German Democratic Republic of yesteryear.

But even in the exceptional case that all requirements are met, that does not guarantee that a particular democracy functions as the Ought camp would have it.

Why? I am afraid that once again I have to come back to my main point, my principal argument, and that is the fact that democracy – like all of mankind's institutions – is run by fallible humans.

And not only that. Humanity is not a homogeneous ensemble of generally well-intentioned individuals. It comprises, unfortunately, also less well-meaning, malicious and downright criminal characters. It is no good to believe in a system of government that assumes the goodness of people – the basic error of all utopian, millenarian thinking. It leaves gaping holes in the net through which the bad can slip and perpetrate mischief.

This was precisely what Karl Popper had in mind when he said that the purpose of a good government, rather than anything else, is to prevent the bad and incompetent from doing too much harm.

- 4 -

To identify the shortcomings of democracy is a relatively easy task. So is the analysis of the imperfections of human nature that obstruct the proper functioning of democracy. Quite another thing is to come up with (preventive) remedies.

The first remedy that people invariably come up with is more involvement of the citizenry. This has been tried since time immemorial, without the slightest success. It is rather clear why.

As Geoffrey Wheatcroft formulated concisely in the *Financial Times* of 17th April, 2010:

> Behind all this one may detect the politicians' deformation professionelle, the belief that everyone is, or ought to be, as interested in politics as its practitioners, and as keen to participate. But this is not so, and there is no reason why it should be.

The primacy of politics in other words, which is preached so ardently by politicians but also by all those who gravitate to the sphere of political life, the political arena: journalists, columnists, pundits, academics, party workers and the like.

The ordinary citizen, the average voter, has however other pressing concerns than politics. The Ancient Greeks may well have branded a citizen who did not take part in political life as an "*idiotis*", but note that this concerned only Athenian citizens who constituted a limited percentage of the total population. This citizen had free time to spare—slaves would take care of most of the work—so for him it was no great sacrifice to devote part of his time to political activity. On the contrary he did so with great gusto.

Present-day citizens, I believe, do not want to govern themselves. They want the tasks of government to be carried out by their representatives, whom they have elected for that very purpose.

Government of the people — for sure; government for the people — definitely; but not necessarily government by the people.

Nowadays life is considerably more complicated than in Ancient Greece, requiring amounts of time and energy that our Athenian citizen probably would have difficulty imagining.

One may lament the lack of involvement of people, but one cannot force them to take part in the political rituals if they are not so inclined — that would be undemocratic anyway. The choice is theirs, and they are at liberty to exercise their right to vote or not. Even if when they choose not to that choice will not please those who think they are badly mistaken.

- 5 -

I conclude with a few thoughts that could perhaps help to put democracy in perspective. First of all there was, I repeat, Churchill who perspicaciously observed that "It has been said that democracy is the worst form of government, except all those that have been tried from time to time." That begs the question whether possibly at some time in the future man will find a better way. I have my doubts — in fact, I am sure man will not.

Democracy for all its shortcomings is still, and is likely to remain, the system of government best adapted to man's imperfect nature.

Secondly, I admit that my criticisms of the "Ought camp" were not always entirely fair. I have to recognize the role of normative thinking when it comes to put the finger on "what is wrong and what should be better". Having said that, I think the "Oughts" should realize that real improvement can only be achieved by trial-and-error and (Popperian) piecemeal engineering. Perhaps they should let themselves be inspired by what Kant called a hypothetical imperative, which he defines as the "practical necessity of a possible action as a means to achieve something that one wills".[18] In other words, if one wants to attain a particular goal, one needs to perform a specific action. So — if one wants "bad and incompetent people (not) to do too much harm", one needs to take specific appropriate measures to stop them.

The existing framework of laws, rules and regulations does protect the citizen and institutions to a large extent. But that net — similar to all human creations — is not perfect. Gaps and breaches develop as a natural occurrence, and through the holes the villains slip. Every gap, every breach, once discovered demands to be fixed: a specific measure to achieve a specific goal. Such repair jobs are a constant in our imperfect world. Piecemeal engineering again, indeed.

Repairs to the net are, by definition, ex-post. But as yet undefined potential dangers may lurk in the recesses of the future: the "unknown unknowns". Who could, for instance, have expected some 40 years ago when the internet appeared on the scene that cybercrime would become a serious threat? Or to pick on the world of finance, nobody foresaw that mortgage-backed securities would be one of the causes of the 2008 financial disasters.

The "unknown unknowns" cannot be neutralized ex-ante. The best one can do is to keep the existing framework of laws and rules under constant surveillance, ready to act when the first signs of cracks appear. It is, however, an illusion to think that one could design a "waterproof" system.

Democracy is, and will remain, a work in progress.

A last remark: democracy is not an end in itself. It is a means to an end and that end is liberty. As Scruton said: "To put the matter bluntly, democracy has no intrinsic value."[19] The value of democracy is instrumental in the sense that, with all its shortcomings, it is, so far, still the best possible system of government to allow the individual to achieve his liberty, his autonomy.

In the end, the ultimate end, each individual seeks to be free, to be the "master of his own fate". And this is what politics, what democracy, should be about.

As Hannah Arendt put it, "The meaning of politics is freedom."[20]

Notes

Preface

1 Speech in the House of Commons, November 1917
2 Isaiah Berlin, *Against the Current* (1979), edited by Henry Hardy, London: Pimlico (1997), p. 120.
3 Oxford University Press (1969), 1988, pp. lv–lvi.

The State

1 Robert Nozick, *Anarchy, State and Utopia*, Oxford: Basil Blackwell (1974), ed. 1988, p. 3.
2 Nozick, *ibid.*, p. 4.
3 Thomas Hobbes, *Leviathan* (1654), London: Penguin Classics, ed. 1985, pp. 185–186.
4 Jean-Jacques Rousseau, *Du contrat social* (1762), Paris: Garnier Flammarion, ed. 1966.
5 I have a problem with his identification of freedom with the "*Volonté Générale*" and he has lost me when he argues that "whoever refuses to obey the General Will will be forced by the entire community; which means nothing else than that he will be forced to be free" (*Contrat social*, Livre I, Chapitre VII; own translation). Even more puzzling I find his apparent disdain

for the people (which he nonetheless considers capable of concluding a *Contrat social*) when it comes to making laws: "How can a blind crowd, which often does not know what it wants because it rarely knows what is good for it, perform itself such a difficult task as the designing of a legislative system?" (Livre II, Chapitre VI; own translation). To do this job he introduces a *deus ex machina*: "… a supreme intelligence, a legislator." This "extraordinary man in the State" would seem to act as a consultant. He drafts the laws, but has "no legislative rights", which rest with the people only. The legislator subsequently disappears without leaving a trace in the remaining text of the *Contrat social*. I have some sympathy with Scruton when he says of the *Contrat social* that "the work is unsystematic and fraught with paradoxes. It can be read either as a celebration of liberty and the rights of man, which condemns all forms of absolute or arbitrary government, or as a recipe for the abolition of human liberties and the absorption of the individual into a sovereign collective." He continues to say that "Nevertheless its fundamental conceptions have been highly influential and its very contradictory nature has often been esteemed as the mark of vision that recognizes the contradictions implicit in all social order" (Roger Scruton, *A Dictionary of Political Thought*, London: Pan Books, 1983, p. 414).

[6] Wherever in this text I speak of men, I mean mankind, i.e. including women.

7 I have no use for any thought experiment that invokes it, or for the term "thought experiment". An experiment is, according the *Concise Oxford Dictionary*, "(i) a procedure adopted on the chance of its succeeding for testing a hypothesis etc., or to demonstrate a known fact (2) a test or trial." There is here obviously no question of testing a hypothesis, or of a test or trial. I propose, instead, the term "hypothetical case study".

8 London: Profile Books (2011).

9 Fukuyama, *ibid.*, p. 30.

10 Jesse Norman, *Edmund Burke: The First Conservative*, New York: Basic Books (2013), p. 200.

11 Fukuyama, *ibid.*, p. 15.

12 Nozick, *ibid.*, p. ix.

13 Quotes from Karl Popper, *The Open Society and Its Enemies* (1945), London: Routledge, ed. 1987, vol. 2, p. 31.

14 James M. Buchanan, *Constitutional Economics*, Oxford: Basil Blackwell (1991), p. 8.

15 Immanuel Kant, *Zum ewigen Frieden. Ein philosophischer Entwurf* (1795), Stuttgart: Philipp Reclam jun., ed. 1984, p. 31 (own translation).

16 Karl Popper, *The Open Society and Its Enemies*, vol. 1, p. 121.

17 Karl Popper, *ibid.*, pp. 263–264. Montesquieu held similar views.

18 Machiavelli, once again, being the most obvious example.

19 The Rule of Law of course also protects people against each other.

[20] Mancur Olsen, *Power and Prosperity: Outgrowing Communist and Capitalist Dictatorships*, New York: Basic Books (2000), pp. 195–196.

[21] Mancur Olsen, *ibid.*, p. 196.

[22] Buchanan, *ibid.*, p. 8.

[23] Samuel Brittan, *Capitalism with a Human Face*, Oxford: Basil Blackwell (1991), p. 8.

[24] Joseph Raz, *The Morality of Freedom*, Oxford: Clarendon Press (1986), pp. 5–6.

[25] Roland Dumas in *Le Point* of 10th July 2014 (own translation).

[26] Reinhold Niebuhr, *Moral Man & Immoral Society: A Study in Ethics and Politics* (1932), reprinted, Louisville, KT: Westminster John Knox Press (2001).

Democracy

[1] Thucydides: Pericles Funeral Speech, as quoted in A.N.W. Saunders (ed.) *Greek Political Oratory*, London: Penguin Books, ed. 1987, p. 34.

[2] Plato, *The Republic*, Penguin Classics, ed. 1974, Book VIII 557b, p. 293.

[3] *Carnets*, III, 1958.

[4] Mogens Herman Hansen, *The Athenian Democracy in the Age of Demosthenes*, translated by J.A. Crock, Oxford: Basil Blackwell (1992), pp. 93–94.

[5] Recently the idea has been resuscitated to select a part of the people's representatives by lot (cf. David van Reybrouck, *Tegen Verkiezingen*, Amsterdam: De Bezige Bij, 2013. The title translates as *Against Elections*).

Apparently, it is not a question of abolishing parliamentary elections, but to supplement the existing legislature by a forum of citizens chosen by lot. This would help to raise the involvement of the population in political life.

I have my doubts. The shortcomings of democracy are not going to be alleviated by the random appointment of a number of citizens. To suppose that this assembly will act differently, more sensibly than a regular parliament, is unlikely in my opinion. It will only complicate political life further without resulting in any additional benefits.

6   Hansen, *ibid.*, p. 313.

7   In a book blurb the Princeton University Press called it no less than "the most widely debated conception of democracy in recent years."

8   The German original dates from 1981, an English edition was published by Beacon Press (Boston, MA) in 1984 (translated by Thomas McCarthy)

9   His major work on the subject is *Between Facts and Norms: Contributions to a Discourse Theory of Law and Democracy*, Cambridge, MA: MIT Press (1998), translated by William Rehg. First published in German by Suhrkamp Verlag (Frankfurt am Main), 1992.

10 Cf. Catherine Audard, "Le principe de légitimité démocratique", in Rainer Rochlitz (ed.) *Habermas. L'usage public de la raison*, Paris: Presses Universitaires de France (2002), p. 96.

11 James Gordon Finlayson, *Habermas: A Very Short Introduction*, Oxford: Oxford University Press (2005), p. 44.

[12] *The Economist*, 24th October 1998.

[13] *The Economist*, 21st October 2017.

[14] J.S. Mill, *Considerations on Representative Government* (1861), reprinted, New York: Prometheus Books (1991), p. 97.

Mill was a strong advocate of representative government, but he did not see it as a panacea, he did see its inadequacies as well. He warned against the danger of a "tyranny of the majority" and emphasized "that the dangers incident to a representative democracy are of two kinds: danger of a low grade of intelligence in the representative body (sic!) and in the popular opinion that controls it; and the danger of class legislation on the part of the majority, these being all composed of the same class" (p. 144).

[15] Cf. *Le Contrat social*, Livre III, Chapitre XV.

[16] As quoted in Conor Cruise O'Brian, *The Great Melody: A Thematic Biography of Edmund Burke*, London: Sinclair-Stevenson (1992), p. 75.

[17] Efficacy, according to Raymond Aron, defines "a good policy" (cf. his "Lettre ouverte à un jeune Français en Allemagne", in *Esprit*, February 1933, p. 739).

[18] *The Economist*, Bagehot, 24th February 2001.

[19] Frédéric Worms, *Les Maladies Chroniques de la Démocratie*, Paris: Desclée de Brouwer (2017).

The Political Arena

[1] Baruch de Spinoza, *A Political Treatise* (1670), Mineola, NY: Dover Publications, ed. 2004, p. 288.

2   Spinoza, *ibid.*, p. 287.

3   Jean-Jacques Rousseau, *Discours sur l'origine de l'inégalité* (1754), Paris: Ernest Flammarion Editions, ed. 1931, p. 74 (own translation).

4   Full title: *Discourses on the First Ten Books of Titus Livy*, ed. by Bernard Crick, London: Penguin Books (1970).

5   *Discourses, ibid.*, p. 111 and p. 112.

6   Thomas Hobbes, *Leviathan* (1651), ed. by C.B. Macpherson, London: Penguin Books, ed. 1968, p. 161 and p. 185.

7   Hobbes, *ibid.*, p. 186.

8   Erich Fromm, *Escape from Freedom*, New York: Henry Holt Company (1974), p. 64.

9   *The Cambridge Companion to Gadamer*, ed. by Robert J. Dostal, Cambridge: Cambridge University Press (2002), p. 87.

10   Kai Hammerstein, *Gadamer* (Dutch edition), Rotterdam: Lemniscaat (2002), p. 30.

11   As reported in the Dutch newspaper *Trouw* of 14th March 2002.

12   Graham Wallas, *Human Nature in Politics* (1908), reprinted by Dodo Press (Wokingham), 2011.

13   Daniel Kahneman, *Thinking, Fast and Slow*, London: Allen Lane (2011).

14   Bryan Caplan, *The Myth of the Rational Voter: Why Democracies Choose Bad Policies* (1971), Princeton: Princeton University Press, ed. 2007, p. 3.

15   Harold D. Lasswell, *Psychopathology and Politics* (1930), Chicago, IL: University of Chicago Press Midway Reprint, ed. 1986, p. 46.

16 *Oxford Handbook of Political Psychology*, ed. by David O. Sears, Leonie Huddy and Robert Jervis, Oxford: Oxford University Press (2003), pp. 755–756.

17 Lasswell, *ibid.*, p. XXV.

18 Lasswell, *ibid.*, p. 262.

19 A sweeping assessment that I do not think applies uniformly across the board to each and every politician. There are of course decent people in politics who honestly try to do what is in the public interest — as they perceive it.

20 Harold D. Lasswell, *Politics: Who Gets What, When, How* (1936), New York: Peter Smith, ed. 1950, p. 16.

21 It seems to me that women are less prone to this particular weakness.

22 *N.Y. Herald Tribune*, 25th November 1963.

23 Erich Fromm, *The Anatomy of Human Destructiveness*, (1973), London: Penguin Books, ed. 1990, p. 274.

24 Tom Wolfe, *A Man in Full*, London: Picador (1990), pp. 692–693.

25 London: Michael Joseph (2002).

26 Paxman, *ibid.*, p. 47.

27 London: HarperCollins (2002).

28 Johnson, *ibid.*, pp. 112–113.

29 Matthew Parris, *Chance Witness: An Outsider's Life in Politics*, London: Penguin Books (2003), p. 246.

30 This was meant seriously, I'm afraid. Full text of the interview in the Belgian magazine *Humo* of 14th June 2005.

31 Bernard Mandeville, *The Fable of the Bees* (1714), edited
    by Philip Hart, London: Penguin Books, ed. 1989, pp.
    90–91.

32 Cf. Preface above re Max Weber's *"Gesinnungsethik"*,
    the ethics of good intentions, as opposed to
    "Verantwortungsethik", the ethics of responsibility.

33 In the following I only refer to terrorism inspired by
    ideological principles. Political terrorism as practised
    by such groups as ETA, IRA, Hamas, etc. is, of course,
    of a different nature.

34 In *Humo* magazine, published in two instalments, 25th
    February and 16th September 2003.

35 E.g. Brigate rosse, Lotta Continua, Action Directe,
    CCC, Rote Armee Faktion, Sendero Luminoso,
    Tupamaros et alii.

36 See Vincenzo Tessandori, *Br. Imputazionze: banda
    armata. Cronaca e documenti delle Brigate rosse*, Milan:
    Garzanti (1977). Very good on the Brigate rosse is also
    Robert C Meade Jr, *Red Brigades: The Story of Italian
    Terrorism*, London: Macmillan Press (1990).

37 If I may paraphrase Bernard Crick, *In Defence of
    Politics*.

38 Wolfe's Mayor of Atlanta underestimated this. Or he
    didn't want to admit it.

39 Which makes me think of Andreotti's dictum: "Power
    wears out those who do not have it" (*Il potere logora chi
    non ce l'ha*). Remarkably he wielded power until well
    into his eighties.

[40] Obviously there are politicians who have genuine ideals, who seek power to help achieve a better life for all—but they are, I believe, a minority. Unfortunately.

[41] David Owen, *The Hubris Syndrome: Bush, Blair and the Intoxication of Power*, London: Methuen, revised ed. 2012, and David Owen, *In Sickness and in Power: Illness in Heads of Government During the Last 100 Years*, London: Methuen (2008).

[42] Cardinal Mazarin, *Bréviaire des Politiciens* (1684), Paris: Arléa, ed. 1996, p. 17.

[43] See on this James A. Coloiaco, *ibid.*, especially Chapter 3 "Socrates and Rhetoric", pp. 23–36.

[44] *de Volkskrant* of 6th December 2004.

[45] Simon Hoggart, *Playing to the Gallery*, London: Atlantic Books (2002), p. 157.

[46] John Dunn, *The Cunning of Unreason: Making Sense of Politics*, London: HarperCollins (2000), p. ix.

[47] Buchanan, *ibid.*, p. 9.

[48] Cf. Note #17, Chapter "Democracy".

[49] Samuel Brittan in the *Financial Times* of 20th December 2001.

[50] Raymond Aron, *Introduction à la philosophie politique*, Paris: Le Livre de Poche Editions Le Fallois, ed. 1986, p. 36.

[51] Machiavelli, *The Discourses, ibid.*, p. 113.

[52] C.G. Jung, *Essays on Contemporary Events*, London: Arke Paperbacks (1988), p. 8.

[53] John Dunn, *ibid.*, p. 361.

[54] Luuk van Middelaar, *Politicide. De moord op de politiek in de Franse filosofie* (*Politicide: The Murder of Politics in*

French Philosophy), Amsterdam: Van Gennip (1999), p. 181.

55 Chantal Mouffe, *On the Political*, London: Routledge (20070.

56 Mouffe, *ibid.*, p. 2.

57 Mouffe, *ibid.*, p. 3.

58 Mouffe, *ibid.*, p. 29.

59 Carl Schmitt, *The Concept of the Political* (1932), expanded edition, Chicago, IL: University of Chicago Press (2007), translated by George Schwab, p. 36.

60 Mouffe, *ibid.*, p. 13.

61 A good example of this disconnect between academic philosophy and the reality of political life is Martha Nussbaum's *Political Emotions: Why Love Matters for Justice*, Cambridge, MA: Harvard University Press (2013). She is of course right in insisting that emotions play a role in politics, but it goes a bit too far, I think, to argue that love comes into it. Compare her thesis with what, for instance, Alan Clarke, a former UK Cabinet Minister, had to say: "There are no true friends in politics. We are all sharks circling and waiting for traces of blood to appear in the water" (*Diary*, 30th November 1990).

Conclusion

1 The first because its President is chosen by the Electoral College, while the UK's "first past the post" system can result in a huge discrepancy between the

actual votes for a particular party and its seats in the House of Commons.

2   In 1944/45 Karl Popper published in *Economica* (XI and XII) his essay "The Poverty of Historicism", of which section 24 concerned "Piecemeal Social Engineering". Reprinted in David Millar (ed.) *A Pocket Popper*, London: Fontana Press (1987).

3   Karl Popper, *The Open Society and Its Enemies* (1945), London: Routledge, ed. 1989.

4   Popper, Volume I, *ibid.*, p. 200.

5   Popper Volume 2, *ibid.*, p. 2.

6   Volume 2, *ibid.*, p. 28. On the same page he takes Hegel severely to task about his nonsensical theorizing concerning "the relations between sound and heat". It reminds me of a recent delightfully irreverent book making fun of the pedantic pseudoscientific gobble-degook of some postmodern French and American philosophers and sociologists (Lacan, Baudrillard, Feyerabend, et alii) who without an understanding of what they are talking about make the weirdest use of physics and mathematics to prove a point; Alain Sokal and Jean Bricmont, *Impostures intellectuelles*, Paris: Editions Odile Jacob (1997).

7   Volume 2, *ibid.*, p. 32. To be honest, I have to admit that I find Popper's assault on Hegel rather amusing. I too have been mystified by his writings (as far as I have been able to read them). Moreover, what he says about the state I have problems with (cf. Chapter I, "The State").

8   Volume 2, *ibid.*, p. 33.

9   Volume 2, *ibid.*, p. 82.

10 *Ibid.*

11 Volume 2, *ibid.*, p. 157.

12 *Ibid.*

13 Plato, *The Republic*, 501a.

14 Cf. Isaiah Berlin, *passim*.

15 *The Open Society*, Volume 1, p. 162.

16 Marcus Aurelius, *Meditations*, Book 9, Chapter 20, London: Penguin Classics (2000).

17 Quoted by François Huguenin, *Histoire intellectuelle des droites*, Paris: Perrin (2013), p. 206. The quote is from Tocqueville's *De la démocratie en Amérique*, Tome I.

18 Immanuel Kant, *Groundwork of the Metaphysics of Morals* (*Grundlegung zur Metaphysik der Sitten*, 1785), translated by Mary Gregor, Cambridge: Cambridge University Press, ed. 2003, p. 28.

19 Roger Scruton, *Untimely Tracts*, London: Macmillan (1987), p. 217.

20 Hannah Arendt, *The Promise of Politics*, New York: Schocken Books (2005), p. 108.